Tennis Rules
Copyright 2018 by Brandon Christopher
All rights reserved.
Printed in agreement with Buddy the Ball LLC
10300 W Charleston Blvd 13-A34
Las Vegas, NV 89155
Buddy the Ball and Bella the Ball are trademarks of Buddy
the Ball LLC and its affiliates.

BUDDYTHEBALL.NET

RULES OF TENNIS
STARRING;
BUDDY THE BALL,
BELLA THE BALL,
DIRTY THE DOG,
ROCKY THE RACQUET,
KIERAN THE PRO
AND
CHRISTINA THE COACH.

Written by Brando Christo
Illustrated by Kat Glidewell

Hi friend!
"I'm Buddy the Ball."

I would love to teach you how to play tennis.

It is a really great game with lots of fun and exercise enjoyed all around the world by gazillions of Buddy's friends just like you.

Each tennis court is divided by a big net in the middle. Your job is to hit the tennis ball over the net. You must keep the ball inside the court. You also try to stop your opponent from hitting the ball back to your side of the court. That's when YOU win a point.

"Bark" – Dirty the Dog

Oh right, our friend Dirty the Dog says if you do not hit the ball over the net or if you hit the ball outside the court, you lose the point. Then Dirty the Dog will try to snatch the ball and play a slobbery game called Fetch. "Bark!" Trust me, it's only fun for Dirty. But don't worry, I'm sure you can keep the ball in the court.

"When you win the tennis match you are the champion like me."
-Kieran the Pro.

That's Kieran our favorite tennis pro. He's very competitive. He thinks he's the only one who likes to win. But I'll let you in on a secret. We all like to win.

Playing tennis is most fun when you know the rules. You get to learn the rules right now.

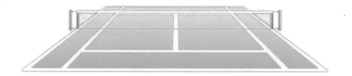

There are two ways to play tennis. One way is called Singles when there is one player on each side of the net. When you play Singles, the ball must not go outside the singles sidelines on the court.

The other way to play tennis is called Doubles where there are two players on each side of the net. When you play Doubles, the ball must not go *outside* the doubles sidelines on the court.

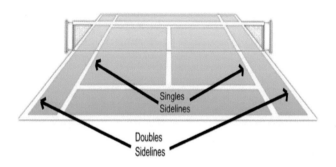

"Remember the racquet!" - Rocky the Racquet.

Right! Rocky the Racquet says each player must use a racquet because if the ball hits your body, you lose the point. Racquets are very cool and are just right to hit the ball. Rocky also says there are different kinds of tennis courts to play on including hard court, grass, clay and carpet.

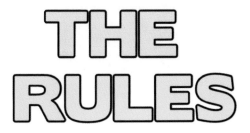

THE RULES

Before the tennis match begins you and your opponent decide who serves the ball first, usually with a heads-or-tails toss of a coin or a spin of your racquet.

The winner decides who serves first or they let the other player decide. The other player then gets to decide which side of the court they want to start on.

SERVING THE BALL

Each player serves for a whole game, then it is the other player's turn. Also, players will switch sides of the court after each odd numbered game: after the first game, the third game, the fifth game, etc.

SCORING
Okay, now it's time to talk about scoring. It can be tricky.

"Don't forget about Love,"
- Bella the Ball.

Our sweetheart, Bella the Ball, reminds you that every game starts with Love. Not the hugging kind of love. Love in tennis means you have no score. Why do we say love? Some think it comes from the French word l'oeuf, which means egg. And a zero on the scoreboard looks like the shape of an egg.

More on scoring. When you score one point, it is called '15". Really? That sounds as strange as the egg story. Remember, each tennis game is played to four points. Think of a clock. Fifteen minutes on a clock is one quarter of the hour. And there are four quarters in an hour. So one point in tennis is called 15. Two points is called "30" because thirty minutes is two quarters of an hour. Three points is called "40" which is almost three-quarters of the hour. And the fourth point is 'game point' which wins the game.

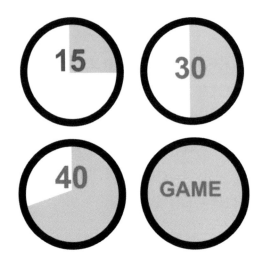

If you are serving and
have three points and your

opponent has two points, the score is 40-30. The server always says their score first. If you are serving and have two points and your opponent has three points the score is 30-40.

If both you and your opponent have three points, that's called "deuce," which means a tie. So it's time to break the tie. The point for the player who scores right after deuce is called 'advantage.' If that player also wins the next point, they win the game. But if you win the next point, the game continues. You see, the game is not over until one player wins two points in a row.

Let's see, fetch, love, clocks, deuce, set. It can be tricky.

THE SERVE

During a game, the server stands behind the baseline on the *right* half of the court. They serve the ball diagonally to the service box on the other player's side of the net. The server gets two chances to get the ball in. If the player misses both serves, they lose the point.

After the ball has been served players can move anywhere they want on their side of the court. When that point is complete a new point begins. The server now moves behind the baseline on the *left* half of the court. Again, the ball is served diagonally to the other service box on the opponent's side of the net. Back and forth. Switching side-to-side after each serve. It is important to remember, that if you step over the baseline before serving the ball, it is a "foot fault "and you lose that serve.

NICKING THE NET

If you serve and the ball nicks the very top of the net but still goes into the proper service box, it is called a "let" and the server makes another serve. But if the ball nicks the net and goes out of the service box, it is called "out" and the serve doesn't count.

Here's a Buddy Quiz: How do you win the game, the set and the match?

WINNING THE GAME
To win a game, a player must win at least four points and two more points than the opponent.

WINNING THE SET

To win a set, a player must play at least six games and also win by two games than the opponent.

WINNING THE MATCH

To win the match, a player must win two-sets-out-of-three. Sometimes they must win three-sets-out-of-five to win the match. (Three-out-of-five set tennis is usually only at Davis Cup matches or in Grand Slam tournaments.)

"Congratulations! You now know the rules of tennis."
-Christina the Coach.

Christina says the more you play tennis the better you will get. And the more fun you will have. You will get great exercise. You will meet new friends.

And you might even want to play with Dirty the Dog if he snatches your tennis ball and asks you to play a slobbery game of Fetch.

So from me to you, Buddy says Bounce Big and Live Bigger.

Shots and Tennis Terms

Winner: A shot that lands inbounds yet the opponent is unable to touch it.

Shank: An unintentional mishit shot that can land either inbounds or out of bounds.

Hook: Cheating in the form of a dirty line call from the opponent. For instance, they call the ball out when really it landed in.

AD In: Advantage (game point) to the server after a deuce point.

AD Out: Advantage (game point) to the returner after a deuce point.

Treeing: When a player is playing so good they might as well have many tree branches extending from their body because they seem to reach every ball.

Spike: A volley smash.

Drop Shot: A shot hit that lands over the net, but so short in the court that if it were to go untouched it would bounce twice before reaching the service line.

Top Spin: Forward spin on the ball.

Slice (Back Spin): Backward spin on the ball.

Kicker: A serve with heavy topspin that causes the ball the "kick up" after bouncing.

Forehand: A one-handed open-palmed swinging groundstroke usually hit with the dominant hand.

Backhand: A one-handed or two-handed closed-palmed swinging groundstroke usually hit the dominant hand or both hands.

Volley: A punching shot that strikes the ball out of the air.

Overhead: A shot like a service motion, but typically in the middle of the court and in the middle of a point.

Line Clipper: A ball that lands inbounds on the line.

Lob: A lofty shot that usually goes above and beyond a players reach/position.

Swinging Volley: A forehand or backhand motion that is hit in the place of a volley to strike the ball out of the air, but with more force than a normal volley.

Follow-through: Extending your hand and racquet from the contact of the ball when hitting towards the target on the other side of the net.

Tweener: A shot hit between the legs.

Slide: Sliding with your feet, usually to make extra effort to get to a ball.

Double fault: Missing two serves in a row which consequents in the loss of point.

Ace: A serve that lands in the service box, but is untouched by the opponent.

Foot fault: When a server steps across the baseline line or the center hash mark during a serve before they contact the ball.

Unforced error: Missing an easy shot.

Forced error: Missing a shot that was difficult as a result of the way the opponent hit the ball.

Printed in Great Britain
by Amazon

19361934R00029